Dear Reader,

My hope is whether you are reading t[illegible]ngst a group of friends, as a family, or in a class[illegible] you cherish the many lessons to be gained from this wonderful story.

As you travel through the pages and meet the characters, be sure to keep your eyes and ears open. This story may challenge your vocabulary so you may want to keep a dictionary close by. Also, per the Queen's request, her APPENDIX OF GOLDEN INFORMATION has been added for your benefit. Make sure you have on your thinking cap because you are certainly going to need it.

There are moments in the story that will take you on an emotional roller coaster, so be prepared. Buckle your seat belt and get ready to embark on a journey you will never forget! On behalf of our Queen, we welcome you to the Land of Zizzamanbee.

Signed,
The Royal Advisor to The Queen (Narrator)

Thinking Cap Warm-ups

(FROM THE QUEEN INFINITY ACTIVITY GUIDE)

1. I am a geometric shape with no corners. I have a center which is always crossed by a diameter. Who am I?
2. Queen Infinity read 33 books in January, 29 books in February, 40 books in March and 35 books in April. What is the average number of books Queen Infinity read per month?
3. The castle's draw bridge is a square. The perimeter of the draw bridge is 38 meters. How long is each side of the bridge?
4. To "take someone under your wing" is an example of which literary device?
5. Stories about fairies or other magical creatures are examples of what type of fiction?

FIND THE ANSWERS AND CHECK OUT THE FREE GLOSSARY AT www.booksbykobie.com.

Queen Infinity

WRITTEN BY L. Kobie Wilkerson
ILLUSTRATED BY Aaron J. Ratzlaff

Love II Learn Books
Atlanta

Queen Infinity is a trademark of Love II Learn Books.

For bulk orders, speaking engagements, or school presentations, contact us at info@booksbykobie.com.

ISBN: 978-0-9796679-1-6 (hardcover)
978-0-9796679-3-0 (paperback)

Library of Congress Control Number: 2011961340

Design by Aaron J. Ratzlaff.
Printed and bound by Palace Press International in China.

First Edition

Visit the official website: www.booksbykobie.com

From Kobie:

Thanks to my mother who showed me the value of reading,
and gave me a love of books.
Thank you for always believing in me and fostering an imagination
that can take me anywhere that I want to go.

A special thank you to the scholars of Ms. Williams 6th grade class (2010) of
Heyward Gibbes Middle School in Richland County School District One.
Thank you for inspiring me and pushing me to finish the letter from
King Radius. I could not have done it without you.

From Aaron:

To Nadia, for keeping my studio lively and myself cheerful.

MY PA
A MACHIN
WHERE IN T
BEEN WORK
THEY'D JUST
THOSE TRANS
THEY WERE
NOISE OF FIGHT
GOING ON INSID
GUARDS GOT IN
THE LAB WAS IN
BE FOUND. THE M
TO BUILD IT, TOO;
COATS, CROWNS, G
I KNOW YOU'RE
THE PART YOU HAVE
MONTHS BEFORE YOU
MY PARENTS SO MUCH
BUT I THINK WHEREVE
THERE TOGETHER.
NOW LET'S GET TO W
BOX AND MORE IMPORT
UNLOCKED. I CREATED T
YOU, AND TO C

Once upon a time in the land of Zizzamanbee lived the prettiest queen of all and her name was Infinity.

Some folks wondered why they called her that. It's because she grew prettier every day—imagine that!

Along with her beauty, her knowledge and wisdom grew too. How it did for sure no one really knew, but we know this is a fact and it's true to be: she had the largest library that you ever did see!

Some speculate and people would say she read a book and sometimes two every single day.

My favorite place

ZIZAX
BOX
SHOP

Every day at noon in Zizzamanbee everyone turned on their zizzabox (*kind of like our TV*) and there they would find Queen Infinity reading a book for all to hear and see.

Everyone (*and I mean everyone*) in Zizzamanbee learned reading was fun, important and key.

This may not be strange to you or anyone else you see, but there is much you don't know about Zizzamanbee.

12:00:00 PM
((LIVE))

What was so strange and what shocked the world is that Queen Infinity was just a small girl.

How old she was exactly I don't rightly know. She was older than 5, but not yet 12 though.

She became Queen at a very young age (*It's a whole OTHER story, and to tell it would take DAYS*).

What I can tell you is:

One night at the stroke of 12, as the belfry on the library was tolling its bells, from the royal chamber they heard a big boom, and when the guards ran into

her parents' room, all they found were their shiny royal shoes. No capes, no clothes, no scepters, no crowns, just their royal shoes and the sheets were turned down.

With her parents gone and being the only child, it was standard law that she'd inherit the crown.

Although sad her parents were gone she stepped up to the plate, and was determined as a Queen she'd do her best to be great!

Even though she was young she ruled her country well. Ask any Zizzamanbean and they'd be quick to tell:

READ
I LOVE the Queen of Zizzamanbee! She does so great by us you see; she sits up high but looks down low...
...and is not full of herself like her uncle you know?!

Her uncle was mean! He was spiteful and openly feared! Her uncle was the King of Eromondear.
His name was King Arrogant and when he said something it's what he meant.
You couldn't tell him he wasn't a genius because he had the power to send you to Venus.

King Arrogant wasn't very tall, and you know what else? His brain was super small!
The love of reading was the exact opposite in his land. There were only a few books in his whole kingdom because reading was banned!
King Arrogant hated reading so much he burned every book he ever read or touched! (*Now between me and you that sounds really bad, but he's read one book his whole life and two's all he's ever had.*)

He considered himself the world's smartest man, simply because he was the smartest man in his land.
He'd stand up and say, ***"YOU ALL LISTEN TO ME! I'M THE SMARTEST MAN THAT COULD EVER BE! I KNOW THE WHOLE ALPHABET FROM A TO P!"*** (*But what your highness didn't know is the alphabet ended with Z.*)

He couldn't tell red from yellow or black from blue, and folks often wondered why he was so confused.

The rumor was:

That was all the schooling he had. We think that's why he's so bitter and mad!
You ask any person who's ever lived in his land, any girl, boy, woman or man,
"Who is your least favorite person on the planet earth? Just yell the name that comes to your mind first."
You could bet your very last cent that ALL of their answers would be:

A simple side note: I think it's important we let it be known that the population of Eromondear is one person and 8 dogs.

Each dog was named a number, so King Arrogant would never have to wonder. 1, 2, 3, 4, 5, 6, 7 and 8, and each number hung off their neck on a shiny gold plate.

There used to be nine dogs that King Arrogant owned,

but an awful thing happened while he was off his throne. King Arrogant went away on a trip for a long time, and while he was gone dog Seven ate Nine. When he returned he was sad to see dog Nine's fate, and so he went from nine dogs down to only eight.

King Arrogant wanted things done his way, and would NEVER (*and I mean NEVER*) listen to what others would say.

This is why there were no people in his land. They all packed up and moved closer to other family and friends.

His citizens would bring him their written concerns, and he'd set their concerns on fire and watch them burn.

"THAT'S WHAT I THINK OF YOUR CONCERNS," he'd say. ***"COME AGAIN ANYTIME AND HAVE A NICE DAY."***

So, King Arrogant was pleased doing things his way, and while walking through the forest on a bright sunny day, he came to a clearing and looked up in a tree and there he saw Queen Infinity.

Sitting in a tree and reading a book, she politely invited her uncle to look.

"I HATE READING AS A MATTER OF FACT, AND EVERYONE AROUND WOULD SWEAR TO THAT!

I CANNOT READ OR SAY THE PROPER VOWELS. I HAD TROUBLE WITH IT GROWING UP AND HAVE THE SAME TROUBLES RIGHT NOW!

ARE YOU TRYING TO MAKE A FOOL OF ME?"

“No, this book has some
incredible pictures
I wanted you to see.”

"I DON'T WANT TO SEE YOUR PICTURES!
I DON'T WANT TO SEE YOUR BOOK!
I DON'T WANT TO HEAR IT,
AND I DON'T WANT TO LOOK!

I DESPISE READING TO THE HIGHEST DEGREE.
YOU'RE LUCKY I DON'T HAVE MY AXE OR I'D
CHOP DOWN THIS TREE. THEN I'D TAKE THE
WOOD AND YOUR PRECIOUS BOOK AND CREATE
A BOMB FIRE SO PEOPLE COULD LOOK. THEN
THEY'D KNOW THAT YOUR BOOK AND TREE
ARE GOOD FOR KINDLING AND NOTHING ELSE.

AND TO THINK, YOU HAVE 1000'S OF BOOKS
UPON YOUR PRETTY GOLDEN SHELVES.

HUH! IT'S FOOLISHNESS, I SAY. IT MAKES ME LAUGH! YOU REMIND ME SO MUCH OF YOUR DAD. HE'D SAY:

I FEEL ALL THAT READING STUFF IS A BUNCH OF CRAP!
YOUR DAD SAID READING WOULD MAKE ME BIG AND I READ ONE BOOK AND IT NEVER DID.
THAT'S WHY I HATE READING SO MUCH, AND I WILL BURN ANY BOOK THAT I WILL EVER TOUCH!"

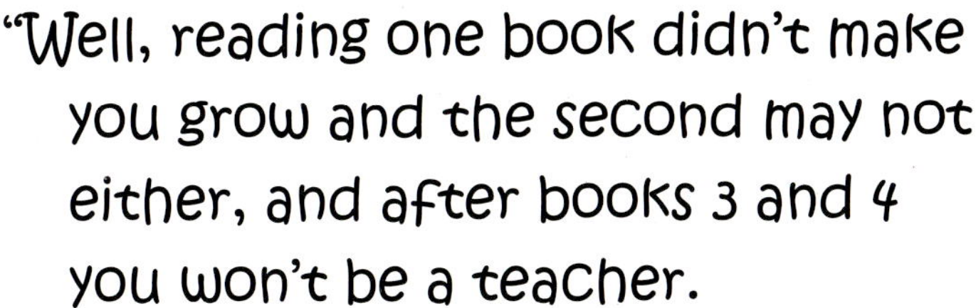

"Well, reading one book didn't make
you grow and the second may not
either, and after books 3 and 4
you won't be a teacher.
Books 5 and 6 may not be
great, and I can't make
any promises about
books 7 and 8.

The important
thing about
reading is that
it is done, but you
may not FEEL any
growth until about
book 101. But that
shouldn't stop you from
reading book number two.
Who knows what can happen
or what you may do?
You may pick up your second book
and something may just click.
For all we know, reading may just be
your gift.

But I can say this for sure, without any
doubt: if you never pick up that second
book you will never find out!

The beautiful thing when you pull a book off a shelf is that you can decide to be someone else.

You can look into new worlds and see what they see and feel what they feel. You can become so engrossed to the point that it all feels real.

You can escape to new places
when everyone's around; a good
book can put your mind in a place
where your body can't be found.

You can be the hero or the villain or neither if you want.

The fact you can put yourself in another's place really is the point.

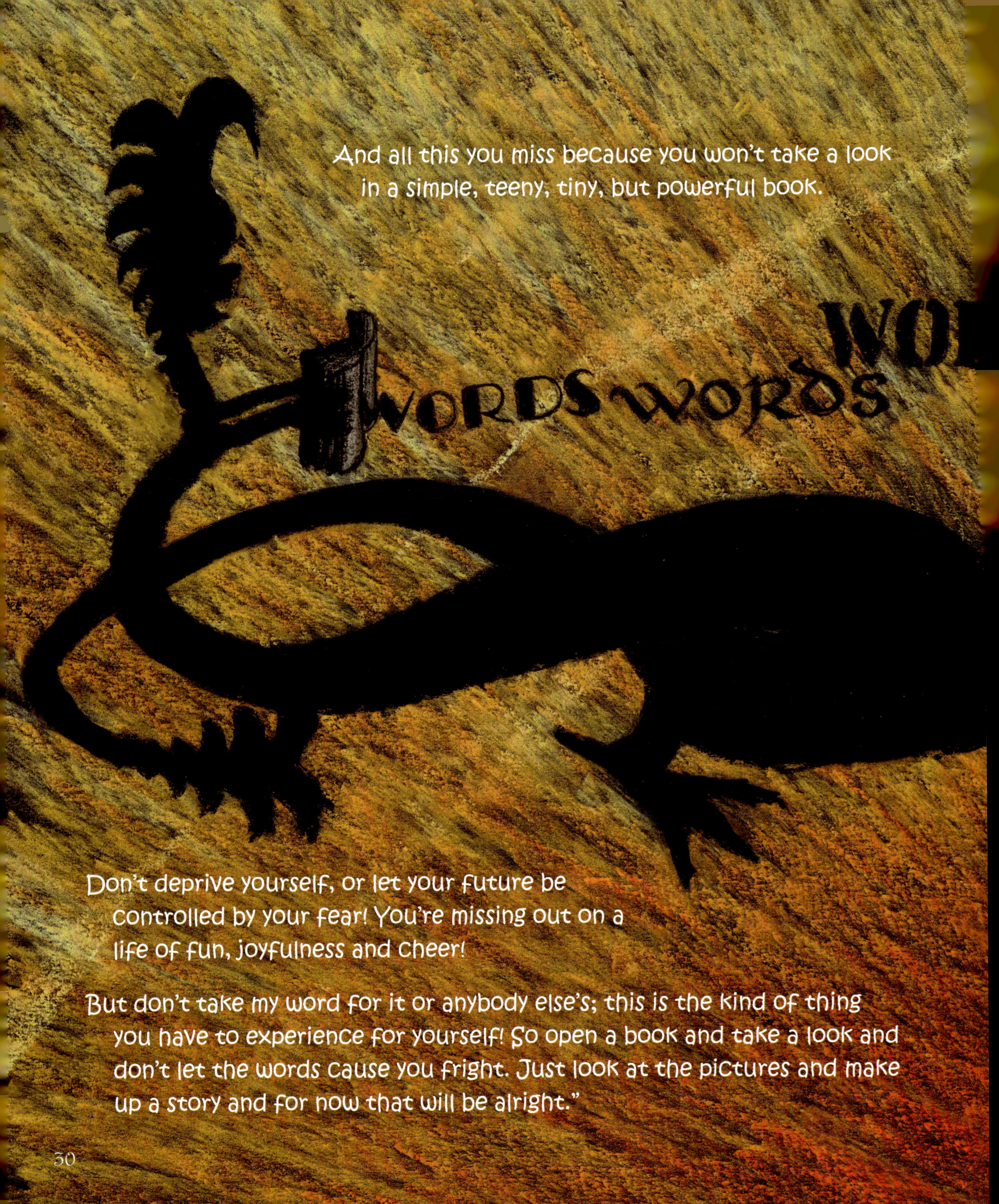

And all this you miss because you won't take a look
in a simple, teeny, tiny, but powerful book.

Don't deprive yourself, or let your future be controlled by your fear! You're missing out on a life of fun, joyfulness and cheer!

But don't take my word for it or anybody else's; this is the kind of thing you have to experience for yourself! So open a book and take a look and don't let the words cause you fright. Just look at the pictures and make up a story and for now that will be alright."

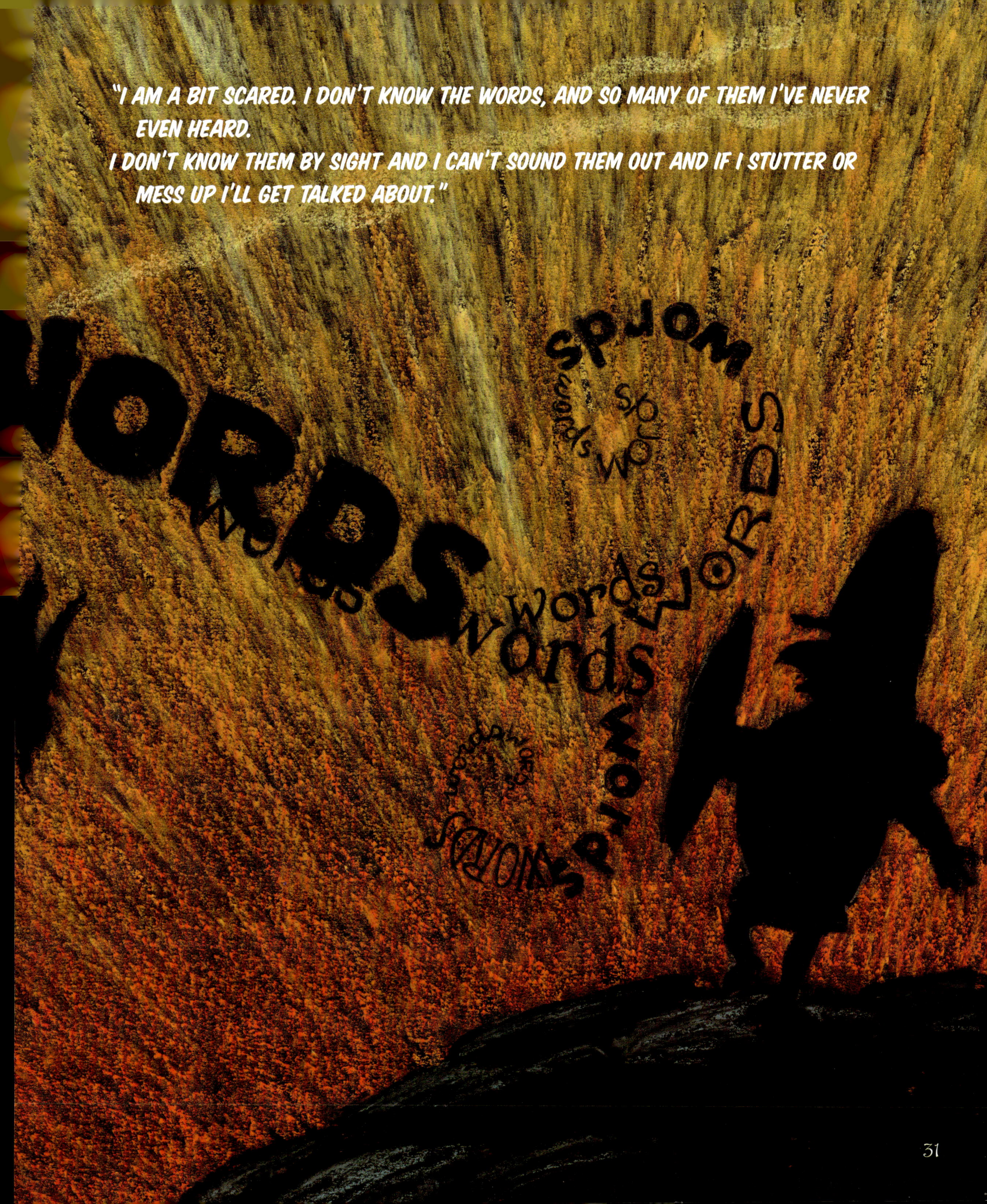
"I AM A BIT SCARED. I DON'T KNOW THE WORDS, AND SO MANY OF THEM I'VE NEVER EVEN HEARD.
I DON'T KNOW THEM BY SIGHT AND I CAN'T SOUND THEM OUT AND IF I STUTTER OR MESS UP I'LL GET TALKED ABOUT."

"I know learning is not your thing, and there's no one in your land,
but if you want help I could give you a hand."

"IT IS TOO LATE FOR ME TO LEARN TO READ, SO I JUST WORK ON BEING MEAN.
SOME HAVE SPORTS, YOU HAVE BOOKS. I INVITE YOU TO GIVE BEING MEAN A SECOND LOOK.
I'VE GOT THIS DOWN TO A SCIENCE YOU KNOW, JUST AS SURE AS GAS COMBUSTION WILL MAKE A CAR GO.
IT COMES FROM WITHIN ME, FROM A PLACE DEEP AND DARK. IT'S LIKE THAT GUY I HEARD YOU ONCE TALK ABOUT ON THE ZIZZABOX: RENE DESCARTES.
I THINK I'M MEAN, THEREFORE I'M MEAN. IT'S MY REALITY IT'S NOT A DREAM!

THE WORLD HAS PROBLEMS, WE KNOW THIS IS TRUE!
FIGURING OUT OUR ROLE IS WHAT WE MUST DO.
SOME PEOPLE FEEL TO CHANGE THE WORLD THAT DOING GOOD
IS THE BEST SOLUTION. I GIVE THEM SOMETHING TO WORK
TOWARDS, THAT'S MY CONTRIBUTION.
I'M THE YIN TO YANG, THE DARK TO THE LIGHT, THE MINUS TO THE PLUS, AND THE
WRONG TO THE RIGHT.
I HAVE PURPOSE AND MY PURPOSE I MUST NURSE. I BRING BALANCE TO THIS
WONDERFUL UNIVERSE.

She waited for him to leave her sight and came
down the tree because it was almost night.
Her feet hit the ground and she ran out the woods,
zooming back to her castle as quickly as she could.

She arrived at her castle nearly out of breath. There was a guy coming down the hill on a contraption to her left.

The guards jumped in front of her and yelled, ***"HALT! You've been warned!"***

And a small voice screamed, "Wait, don't fire! I mean you no harm.

I have a message for the Queen and I've come a long way. I've ridden my plane-a-cycle and it's taken three whole days. Without this machine, my King calculated that five-and-a-half times those days is how long my journey would've taken.

His calculations were true and definitely right. He said I'd arrive on the third day before night. And here I am standing before you and your guards and these beautiful fountains. I come in peace with greetings from my home in the Abacus Mountains.

I have a special message sent from my wise King, which can only be viewed by your wonderful queen."

He pulled out a package that was shaped like a book and gave it to the guards so they could take a look.

They opened the package and inside was a box: a perfect gold cube and on it 5 locks. On one side of the cube there was the numeral one, and under it read ✪PLACE IN THE DIRECTION OF THE SETTING SUN.

"How do I open the box?" asked the Queen.

The messenger shrugged and said, "Beats me!"

"He said to give you the package and you'll know what to do.
Oh, here is a letter and inside are the clues.
He said as much as you read you'll figure it out; you have all the prior knowledge you need with no doubt.
He said this one thing was pertinently necessary: you must open it TONIGHT in the center of your library.
Something about the full moon shining through the top of the dome. Oh, and he said to make sure when you read this letter that you do it alone."

“Well, I have delivered the package and now I’m off. I have my trusty maps for navigation so I won’t get lost.”

He took out a funny shaped bottle and unscrewed his gas tank.

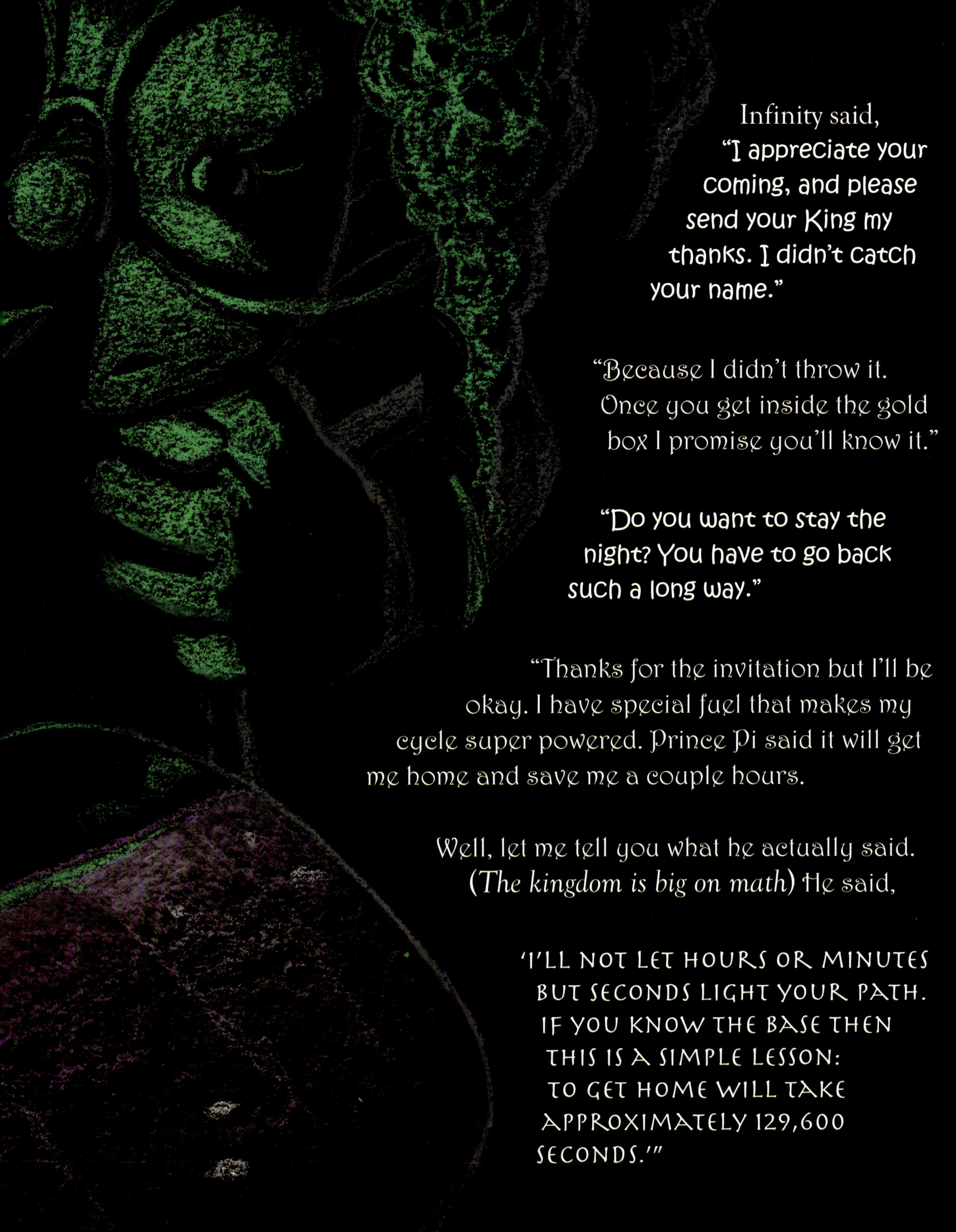

Infinity said,

"I appreciate your coming, and please send your King my thanks. I didn't catch your name."

"Because I didn't throw it. Once you get inside the gold box I promise you'll know it."

"Do you want to stay the night? You have to go back such a long way."

"Thanks for the invitation but I'll be okay. I have special fuel that makes my cycle super powered. Prince Pi said it will get me home and save me a couple hours.

Well, let me tell you what he actually said. (*The kingdom is big on math*) He said,

'I'LL NOT LET HOURS OR MINUTES BUT SECONDS LIGHT YOUR PATH. IF YOU KNOW THE BASE THEN THIS IS A SIMPLE LESSON: TO GET HOME WILL TAKE APPROXIMATELY 129,600 SECONDS.'"

I haven't done the calculations or figured it out in my mind, but I feel like in comparison to get here it'll only take four-eighths the time.
I must be going and get on my way. I know for sure it's going to take me more than a day.
And when I get home I must sleep and shower; the King's birthday party is in exactly forty-eight hours."

Queen Infinity reached under her robe and into her pack and gave him two books to give to his King when he got back.

"My King loves books he'll appreciate these."

And his plane-a-cycle shot off with lightning speed.

Queen Infinity raced through the gates and up to her room. Night had fallen and she could see the rising full moon.

She took off her robe which resembled a cape and ran down the hall to her favorite place.

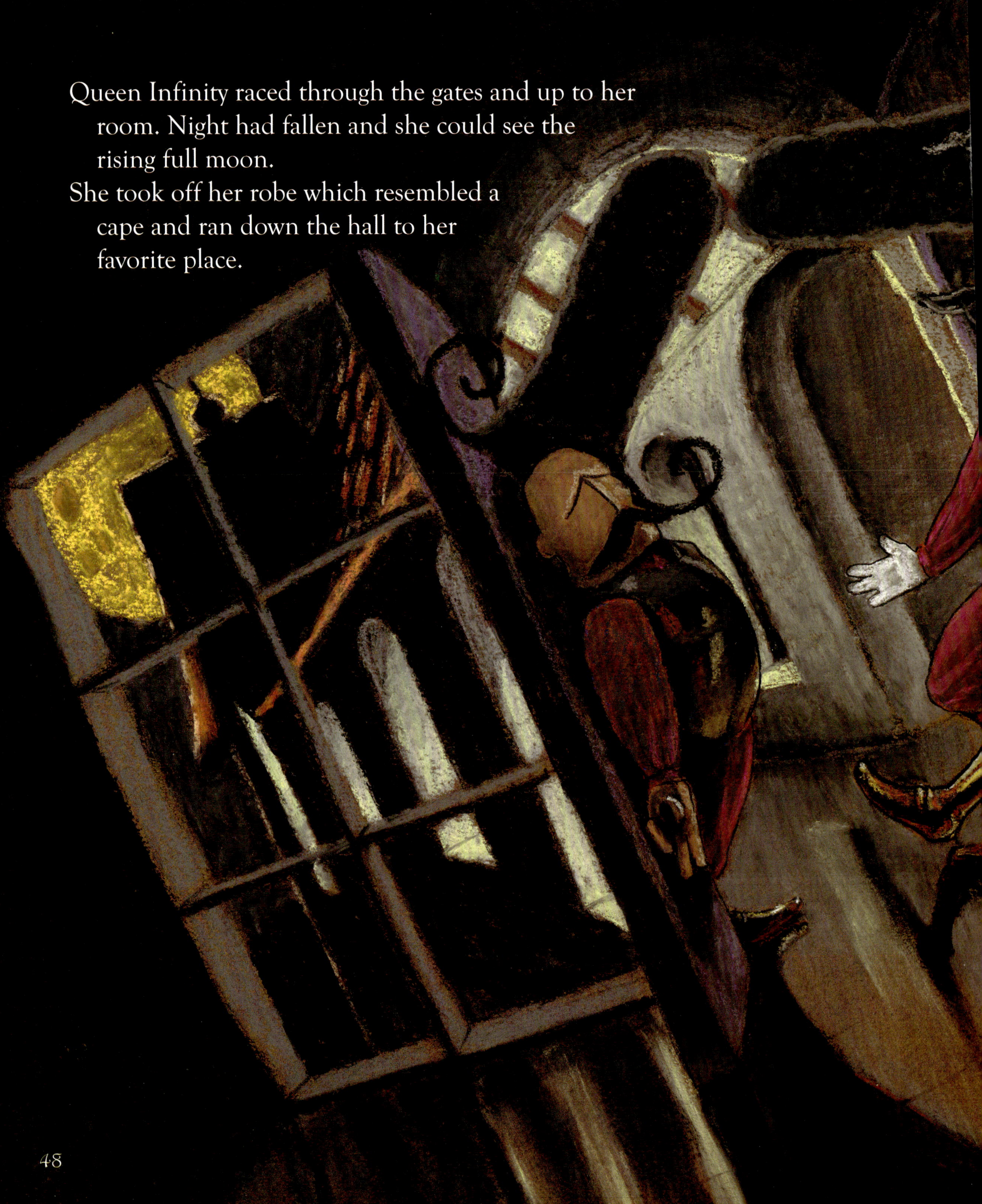

The library guards saw her coming and opened the doors. She slid in on her knees, and to make sure they were closed, she yelled to the guards to be certain she was heard,

She got off her knees with the letter and the cube, then walked to the table in the center of the room.

She put the cube down and put on her thinking sweater, then sat down in the chair and opened the letter.

From the throne  of King Radius

Dear Queen Infinity,

I don't think you'll remember me. I'm about four years older than you, and when I visited with my parents you were only two. Our fathers were friends and I want you to know, my dad felt that friendship is essential to the soul. My parents talked about your parents all the time; I can still hear the stories playing in my mind. Dad said if I ever got in a fix and didn't know what to do, on the faith of their friendship I should reach out to you.

So, I'm reaching out in need of your help; I don't think I can talk to anyone else. We are going to have to sit and talk; I think the disappearance of your parents was my parents' fault. Before you get upset let me explain. I know their loss has caused you great pain. We both share a heavy burden, you and I do; I am a child ruler and my parents are missing too.

My parents were working hard to be the first to create a machine to transport people throughout the universe. They'd been working on it since before I was born, and just got it to where it wouldn't cause those transported any harm.

While running some tests there was a scream from my mom and dad, which prompted the royal guards to charge into the lab. When the guards got inside everything was thrown around; the lab was in ruins and my parents nowhere to be found. The machine was gone and the plans to build it, too. All that was left were their lab coats, crowns, goggles and royal shoes.

I know you're putting it together and this is the part you have to hear: this all happened six months before your parents disappeared. I miss my parents so much and day by day I get better, but I'm sure wherever our parents are, they are there together.

Now let's get to why you have this special box and more importantly how you can get it unlocked. I created that cube especially for you, and to get inside here's what you must do. If all has gone as planned then it should be night. Place the cube in the center on the table to catch the full moon's light.

Remember the directions that were placed on the cube; make sure that is exactly what you do.

It's easy to open the lock at the top. Turn it to this even number and stop: this number is an easy one to figure out; it's the number of teeth in an adult's mouth. If you don't have it, here's what you do: take the atomic number of sulfur and multiply it by 2. Want to know if it's right? This is how you check: it's the same number of bushels in 128 pecks. That number releases a mirror inside the box, and if you get it wrong you can't release the other locks.

Now take that number and multiply it by 4, add up the digits, then add one more. Take that number and divide by three and a single digit is what it should be. To see if you got the real deal, check the hour hand on the clock on the back of a hundred dollar bill. That number will unlock the eastside of the box.

Now let's go counter clockwise and deal with that lock.

Take the number that unlocks the top and multiply it by 8; take the square root of that number and then wait. When the light hits the mirror take the square root one more time, and then take that number and multiply by nine. Now to check if you're right here's how you see: Lyndon Baines Johnson or find a piano and count the black keys.

Now let's move to the opposite pole. Here is the number you're needing to know. Take the numeral engraved on the box, and add it to the number that unlocks the top lock. Then add the number that unlocks the east, and add to that number 33. That's the number you will need to know. Now you have only one more lock to go.

Take the number that opens the south, subtract 10 and you'll have it all figured out.

To check if you're correct, here is the clue: it is the number of drops in a teaspoon. If the answer you still can't muster, it's the number of votes it takes to end a filibuster.

With those numbers you can remove the lid.

And that is exactly what she did! She picked up the top and looked inside the box. She was surprised to see a magnificent watch.

There was writing and a picture on the bottom of the lid. It said DESIGNED BY SEÑOR CUANTIOSO AS A SPECIAL GIFT.

She did a double take and looked at it twice, and it was a sketch of the guy who came on the funny bike.

She put on the watch, it was as light as a feather, then she continued reading and finished the letter.

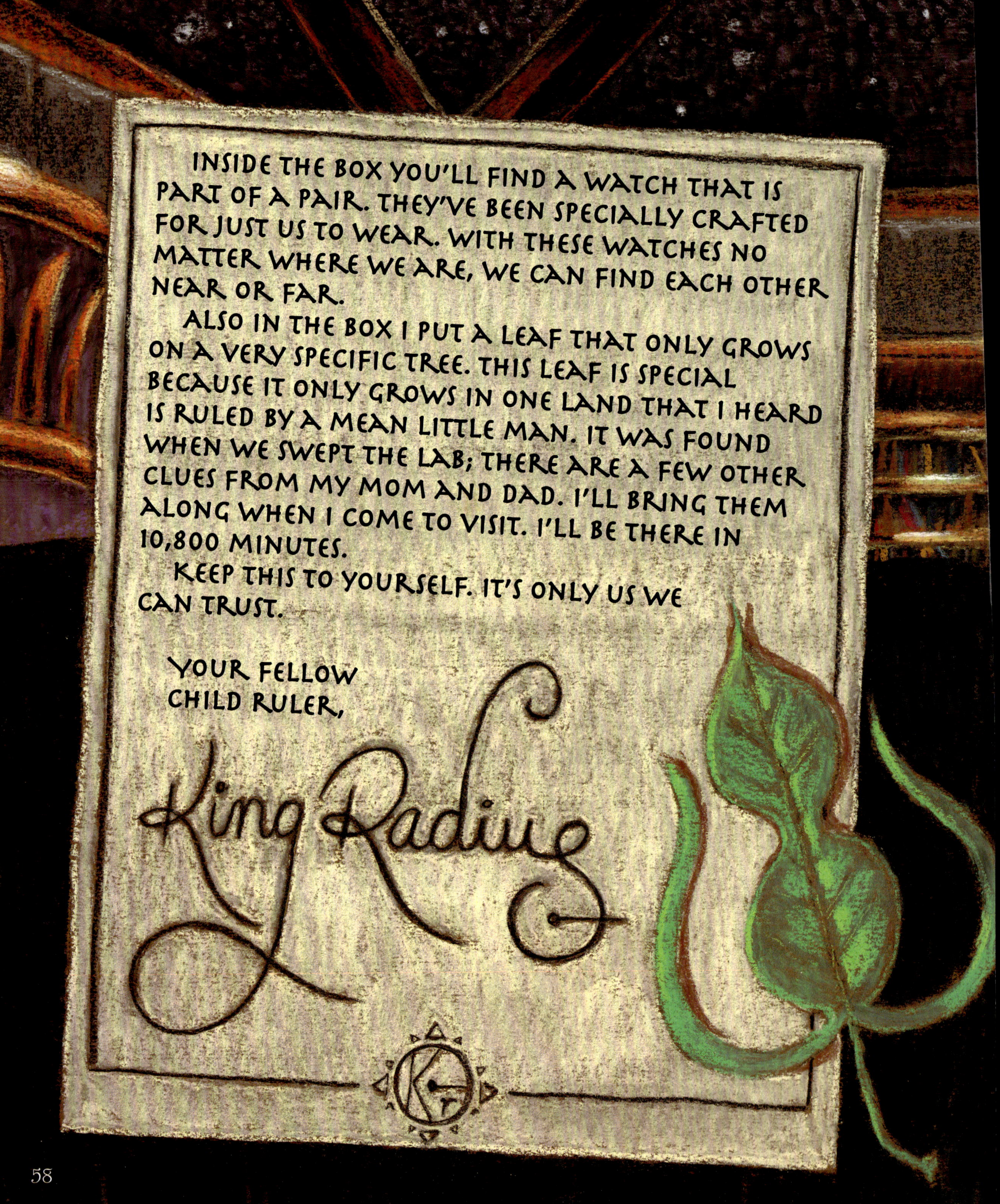

INSIDE THE BOX YOU'LL FIND A WATCH THAT IS PART OF A PAIR. THEY'VE BEEN SPECIALLY CRAFTED FOR JUST US TO WEAR. WITH THESE WATCHES NO MATTER WHERE WE ARE, WE CAN FIND EACH OTHER NEAR OR FAR.

ALSO IN THE BOX I PUT A LEAF THAT ONLY GROWS ON A VERY SPECIFIC TREE. THIS LEAF IS SPECIAL BECAUSE IT ONLY GROWS IN ONE LAND THAT I HEARD IS RULED BY A MEAN LITTLE MAN. IT WAS FOUND WHEN WE SWEPT THE LAB; THERE ARE A FEW OTHER CLUES FROM MY MOM AND DAD. I'LL BRING THEM ALONG WHEN I COME TO VISIT. I'LL BE THERE IN 10,800 MINUTES.

KEEP THIS TO YOURSELF. IT'S ONLY US WE CAN TRUST.

YOUR FELLOW
CHILD RULER,

King Radius

She took the letter and the cube and put them in the safe; it was hidden in one of the golden shelves (*a great hiding place*).

She took off her sweater and laid it on the back of a chair, and thought she couldn't wait for King Radius to get there.

The moon was shining extra bright, and the bookshelves reflected a special gold light.

With her gift on her wrist and the riddle solved her day could now end. She skipped down the hall from her favorite place excited to have a new friend.

She put on her night clothes and took her royal shoes off her feet, said her prayers and then laid down to sleep.

To be continued...

Appendix of Golden Information

Contents

Literature

LITERARY DEVICES

Allegory - A symbolic representation. *Example: The blindfolded figure with scales is an allegory of justice.*
Alliteration - The repetition of the initial consonant. *Example: Peter Piper picked a peck of pickled peppers.*
Allusion - A reference to a famous person or event in life or literature. *Example: She is as pretty as the Mona Lisa.*
Analogy - The comparison of two pairs which have the same relationship. *Example: shoe is to foot as tire is to wheel.*
Assonance - The repetition of similar vowel sounds in a sentence. *Example: The purple bird perched on a curtain.*
Climax - The turning point of the action in the plot of a play or story.
Foreshadowing - Hints of what is to come in the action of a play or a story.
Hyperbole - A figure of speech involving exaggeration, not to be taken literally. *Example: That boy could outrun a cheetah.*
Idiom - An expression that means something other than the literal meaning of the words. *Example: Caught in a jam or a fix.*
Metaphor - A comparison in which one thing is said to be another. *Example: The cat's eyes were jewels, gleaming in the darkness.*
Onomatopoeia - The use of words to imitate the sounds they describe. *Example: The burning wood crackled and hissed.*
Oxymoron - Putting two contradictory words together. *Examples: bittersweet, jumbo shrimp, and act naturally.*
Personification - Giving human qualities to animals or objects. *Example: The daffodils nodded their yellow heads.*
Pun - Use of a word or phrase that suggests two meanings at the same time. *Example: The camera thief took all the pictures.*
Simile - A comparison between unlike things using *like*, *as*, or *as though*. *Example: She floated in like a cloud.*

LITERARY GENRES

FICTION - TEXT THAT DESCRIBES IMAGINARY EVENTS AND PEOPLE.

Drama - Stories where conflicts and emotion are expressed through dialogue and action.
Fable - Narration demonstrating a useful truth, especially in which animals speak as humans.
Fairy Tale - Story about fairies or other magical creatures.
Fantasy - Story with strange or otherworldly settings and characters.
Fiction in Verse - Full-length novels in which the narrative is presented in verse form.
Folklore - The songs, stories, myths, and proverbs of a people as handed down by word of mouth.
Historical Fiction - Story with fictional characters and events in a historical setting.
Horror - Story in which events evoke a feeling of dread in both the characters and the reader.
Humor - Story full of fun, fancy, and excitement, meant to entertain.
Legend - Story, sometimes of a national or folk hero, which has a basis in fact but also includes imaginative material.
Mystery - Story dealing with the solution of a crime or the unraveling of secrets.
Mythology - Legend or traditional narrative, often based in part on historical events, that reveals human behavior and natural phenomena by its symbolism; often pertaining to the actions of the gods.
Poetry - Verse and rhythmic writing with imagery that creates emotional responses.
Realistic Fiction - Story that could actually happen and is true to life.
Science Fiction - Story based on actual, imagined, or potential science, usually set in the future or on other planets.
Short Story - Story of such brevity that it supports no subplots.
Tall Tale - Humorous story with blatant exaggerations and heroes who do the impossible.

NONFICTION - INFORMATIONAL TEXT DEALING WITH A REAL-LIFE SUBJECT.

Biography/Autobiography - Narrative of a person's life; a true story about a real person.
Essay - A short literary composition that reflects the author's outlook or point.
Narrative Nonfiction - Factual information presented in a format which tells a story.
Speech - Public address or discourse.

Numbers

NUMBER NAMES

Number	Name
100	one hundred
1,000	one thousand
10,000	ten thousand
100,000	one hundred thousand
1,000,000	one million
1,000,000,000	billion
1 with 12 zeros	trillion
1 with 15 zeros	quadrillion
1 with 18 zeros	quintillion
1 with 21 zeros	sextillion
1 with 24 zeros	septillion
1 with 27 zeros	octillion
1 with 100 zeros	googol
1 with a googol of zeros	googolplex

ROMAN NUMERALS

I = 1	
V = 5	$\overline{V}$ = 5,000
X = 10	$\overline{X}$ = 10,000
L = 50	$\overline{L}$ = 50,000
C = 100	$\overline{C}$ = 100,000
D = 500	$\overline{D}$ = 500,000
M = 1,000	$\overline{M}$ = 1,000,000

Examples

1 = I	11 = XI	21 = XXI
2 = II	12 = XII	25 = XXV
3 = III	13 = XIII	30 = XXX
4 = IV	14 = XIV	40 = XL
5 = V	15 = XV	49 = XLIX
6 = VI	16 = XVI	51 = LI
7 = VII	17 = XVII	60 = LX
8 = VIII	18 = XVIII	70 = LXX
9 = IX	19 = XIX	80 = LXXX
10 = X	20 = XX	90 = XC

SI (INTERNATIONAL SYSTEM OF UNITS) PREFIXES

Number	Prefix	Symbol
10^{1}	deka-	da
10^{2}	hecto-	h
10^{3}	kilo-	k
10^{6}	mega-	M
10^{9}	giga-	G
10^{12}	tera-	T
10^{15}	peta-	P
10^{18}	exa-	E
10^{21}	zeta-	Z
10^{24}	yotta-	Y

Number	Prefix	Symbol
10^{-1}	deci-	d
10^{-2}	centi-	c
10^{-3}	milli-	m
10^{-6}	micro-	µ (mu)
10^{-9}	nano-	n
10^{-12}	pico-	p
10^{-15}	femto-	f
10^{-18}	atto-	a
10^{-21}	zepto-	z
10^{-24}	yocto-	y

FRACTIONS

Number	Name	Fraction
.1	tenth	1/10
.01	hundredth	1/100
.001	thousandth	1/1000
.0001	ten thousandth	1/10000
.00001	hundred thousandth	1/100000

Mathematics

ADDITION TABLE

+	0	1	2	3	4	5	6	7	8	9	10	11	12
0	0	1	2	3	4	5	6	7	8	9	10	11	12
1	1	2	3	4	5	6	7	8	9	10	11	12	13
2	2	3	4	5	6	7	8	9	10	11	12	13	14
3	3	4	5	6	7	8	9	10	11	12	13	14	15
4	4	5	6	7	8	9	10	11	12	13	14	15	16
5	5	6	7	8	9	10	11	12	13	14	15	16	17
6	6	7	8	9	10	11	12	13	14	15	16	17	18
7	7	8	9	10	11	12	13	14	15	16	17	18	19
8	8	9	10	11	12	13	14	15	16	17	18	19	20
9	9	10	11	12	13	14	15	16	17	18	19	20	21
10	10	11	12	13	14	15	16	17	18	19	20	21	22
11	11	12	13	14	15	16	17	18	19	20	21	22	23
12	12	13	14	15	16	17	18	19	20	21	22	23	24

MULTIPLICATION TABLE

x	1	2	3	4	5	6	7	8	9	10	11	12	13	14	15
1	1	2	3	4	5	6	7	8	9	10	11	12	13	14	15
2	2	4	6	7	10	12	14	16	18	20	22	24	26	28	30
3	3	6	9	12	15	18	21	24	27	30	33	36	39	42	45
4	4	8	12	16	20	24	28	32	36	40	44	48	52	56	60
5	5	10	15	20	25	30	35	40	45	50	55	60	65	70	75
6	6	12	18	24	30	36	42	48	54	60	66	72	78	84	90
7	7	14	21	28	35	42	49	56	63	70	77	84	91	98	105
8	8	16	24	32	40	48	56	64	72	80	88	96	104	112	120
9	9	18	27	36	45	54	63	72	81	90	99	108	117	126	135
10	10	20	30	40	50	60	70	80	90	100	110	120	130	140	150
11	11	22	33	44	55	66	77	88	99	110	121	132	143	154	165
12	12	24	36	48	60	72	84	96	108	120	132	144	156	168	180
13	13	26	39	52	65	78	91	104	117	130	143	156	169	182	195
14	14	28	42	56	70	84	98	112	126	140	154	168	182	196	210
15	15	30	45	60	75	90	105	120	135	150	165	180	195	210	225

PERFECT SQUARES

$1^2 = 1$
$2^2 = 4$
$3^2 = 9$
$4^2 = 16$
$5^2 = 25$
$6^2 = 36$
$7^2 = 49$
$8^2 = 64$
$9^2 = 81$
$10^2 = 100$
$11^2 = 121$
$12^2 = 144$
$13^2 = 169$
$14^2 = 196$
$15^2 = 225$
$16^2 = 256$
$17^2 = 289$
$18^2 = 324$
$19^2 = 361$
$20^2 = 400$
$21^2 = 441$
$22^2 = 484$
$23^2 = 529$
$24^2 = 576$
$25^2 = 625$

Science

PERIODIC TABLE OF THE ELEMENTS

8	← Atomic Number
O	← Chemical Symbol
OXYGEN	← Chemical Name
15.999	← Atomic Weight

KEY
- ■ = solid
- ■ = liquid
- □ = gas

METALS

NON-METALS

1 H HYDROGEN 1.0079																	2 He HELIUM 4.0026
3 Li LITHIUM 6.941	4 Be BERYLLIUM 9.0122											5 B BORON 10.811	6 C CARBON 12.011	7 N NITROGEN 14.007	8 O OXYGEN 15.999	9 F FLUORINE 18.998	10 Ne NEON 20.180
11 Na SODIUM 22.990	12 Mg MAGNESIUM 24.305											13 Al ALUMINUM 26.982	14 Si SILICON 28.086	15 P PHOSPHORUS 30.974	16 S SULFUR 32.065	17 Cl CHLORINE 35.453	18 Ar ARGON 39.948
19 K POTASSIUM 39.0983	20 Ca CALCIUM 40.078	21 Sc SCANDIUM 44.956	22 Ti TITANIUM 47.867	23 V VANADIUM 50.942	24 Cr CHROMIUM 51.996	25 Mn MANGANESE 54.938	26 Fe IRON 55.845	27 Co COBALT 58.933	28 Ni NICKEL 58.693	29 Cu COPPER 63.546	30 Zn ZINC 65.38	31 Ga GALLIUM 69.723	32 Ge GERMANIUM 72.64	33 As ARSENIC 74.922	34 Se SELENIUM 78.96	35 Br BROMINE 79.904	36 Kr KRYPTON 83.798
37 Rb RUBIDIUM 85.468	38 Sr STRONTIUM 87.62	39 Y YTTRIUM 88.906	40 Zr ZIRCONIUM 91.224	41 Nb NIOBIUM 92.906	42 Mo MOLYBDENUM 95.96	43 Tc TECHNETIUM [98]	44 Ru RUTHENIUM 101.07	45 Rh RHODIUM 102.91	46 Pd PALLADIUM 106.42	47 Ag SILVER 107.87	48 Cd CADMIUM 112.41	49 In INDIUM 114.82	50 Sn TIN 118.71	51 Sb ANTIMONY 121.76	52 Te TELLURIUM 127.60	53 I IODINE 126.90	54 Xe XENON 131.29
55 Cs CESIUM 132.91	56 Ba BARIUM 137.33		72 Hf HAFNIUM 178.49	73 Ta TANTALUM 180.95	74 W TUNGSTEN 183.84	75 Re RHENIUM 186.21	76 Os OSMIUM 190.23	77 Ir IRIDIUM 192.22	78 Pt PLATINUM 195.08	79 Au GOLD 196.97	80 Hg MERCURY 200.59	81 Tl THALLIUM 204.38	82 Pb LEAD 207.2	83 Bi BISMUTH 208.98	84 Po POLONIUM [209]	85 At ASTATINE [210]	86 Rn RADON [222]
87 Fr FRANCIUM [223]	88 Ra RADIUM [226]		104 Rf RUTHERFORDIUM [267]	105 Db DUBNIUM [268]	106 Sg SEABORGIUM [271]	107 Bh BOHRIUM [272]	108 Hs HASSIUM [270]	109 Mt MEITNERIUM [276]	110 Ds DARMSTADTIUM [281]	111 Rg ROENTGENIUM [280]	112 Cn COPERNICIUM [285]	113 Uut UNUNTRIUM [284]	114 Uuq UNUNQUADIUM [289]	115 Uup UNUNPENTIUM [288]	116 Uuh UNUNHEXIUM [293]	117 Uus UNUNSEPTIUM [294]	118 Uuo UNUNOCTIUM [294]

57 La LANTHANUM 138.91	58 Ce CERIUM 140.116	59 Pr PRASEODYMIUM 140.91	60 Nd NEODYMIUM 144.24	61 Pm PROMETHIUM [145]	62 Sm SAMARIUM 150.36	63 Eu EUROPIUM 151.96	64 Gd GADOLINIUM 157.25	65 Tb TERBIUM 158.93	66 Dy DYSPROSIUM 162.50	67 Ho HOLMIUM 164.93	68 Er ERBIUM 167.26	69 Tm THULIUM 168.93	70 Yb YTTERBIUM 173.054	71 Lu LUTETIUM 174.97
89 Ac ACTINIUM [227]	90 Th THORIUM 232.04	91 Pa PROTACTINIUM 231.04	92 U URANIUM 238.03	93 Np NEPTUNIUM [237]	94 Pu PLUTONIUM [244]	95 Am AMERICIUM [243]	96 Cm CURIUM [247]	97 Bk BERKELIUM [247]	98 Cf CALIFORNIUM [251]	99 Es EINSTEINIUM [252]	100 Fm FIRMIUM [257]	101 Md MENDELEVIUM [258]	102 No NOBELIUM [259]	103 Lr LAWRENCEIUM [262]

UNITS OF MEASUREMENT

Length

1 foot (ft)	=	12 inches
1 yard (yd)	=	3 ft
1 mile (mi)	=	5280 ft

Dry Volume

1 bushel (bu)	=	4 pk
1 peck (pk)	=	2 (dry) gal

Liquid Volume

1 teaspoon (tsp)	=	60 drops
1 tablespoon (Tbsp)	=	3 tsp
1 fluid ounce (fl oz)	=	2 Tbsp
1 cup (cp)	=	8 fl oz
1 pint (pt)	=	2 cp
1 quart (qt)	=	2 pt
1 gallon (gal)	=	4 qt

SCIENTIFIC CLASSIFICATION

Group Name*	Example: Dog	Example: Human
Kingdom	Animalia	Animalia
Phylum	Chordata	Chordata
Class	Mammalia	Mammalia
Order	Carnivora	Primates
Family	Canidae	Hominidae
Genus	Canis	Homo
Species	Canis Lupus	Homo Sapiens

TIP: *remember the sequence by thinking* King Phillip, Come Out For Goodness Sake!

A.V

Social Studies

PRESIDENTS OF THE UNITED STATES OF AMERICA

1. George Washington, 1789-1797
2. John Adams, 1797-1801
3. Thomas Jefferson, 1801-1809
4. James Madison, 1809-1817
5. James Monroe, 1817-1825
6. John Quincy Adams, 1825-1829
7. Andrew Jackson, 1829-1837
8. Martin Van Buren, 1837-1841
9. William Henry Harrison, 1841
10. John Tyler, 1841-1845
11. James Knox Polk, 1845-1849
12. Zachary Taylor, 1849-1850
13. Millard Fillmore, 1850-1853
14. Franklin Pierce, 1853-1857
15. James Buchanan, 1857-1861
16. Abraham Lincoln, 1861-1865
17. Andrew Johnson, 1865-1869
18. Ulysses Simpson Grant, 1869-1877
19. Rutherford Birchard Hayes, 1877-1881
20. James Abram Garfield, 1881
21. Chester Alan Arthur, 1881-1885
22. Grover Cleveland, 1885-1889
23. Benjamin Harrison, 1889-1893
24. Grover Cleveland, 1893-1897
25. William McKinley, 1897-1901
26. Theodore Roosevelt, 1901-1909
27. William Howard Taft, 1909-1913
28. Woodrow Wilson, 1913-1921
29. Warren Gamaliel Harding, 1921-1923
30. Calvin Coolidge, 1923-1929
31. Herbert Clark Hoover, 1929-1933
32. Franklin Delano Roosevelt, 1933-1945
33. Harry S. Truman, 1945-1953
34. Dwight David Eisenhower, 1953-1961
35. John Fitzgerald Kennedy, 1961-1963
36. Lyndon Baines Johnson, 1963-1969
37. Richard Milhous Nixon, 1969-1974
38. Gerald Rudolph Ford, 1974-1977
39. James Earl Carter, Jr., 1977-1981
40. Ronald Wilson Reagan, 1981-1989
41. George Herbert Walker Bush, 1989-1993
42. William Jefferson Clinton, 1993-2001
43. George Walker Bush, 2001-2009
44. Barack Hussein Obama, 2009-

OUR WORLD: CONTINENTS & OCEANS